MW00448728

# *Wisdom of the*
# VAMPIRES

Lucy Cavendish

*Artwork by Jasmine Becket-Griffith*

**BLUE ANGEL®**
PUBLISHING

# Wisdom of the Vampires

Published by Blue Angel Publishing
80 Glen Tower Drive, Glen Waverley,
Victoria, Australia 3150
E-mail: info@blueangelonline.com
Website: www.blueangelonline.com

Text by Lucy Cavendish
Artwork by Jasmine Becket-Griffith
Edited by Tanya Graham

Blue Angel is a registered trademark of Blue Angel Gallery Pty. Ltd.

ISBN: 978-1-922161-29-1

I will not let you go
into the unknown alone

*Bram Stoker*

# WISDOM OF THE VAMPIRES:
## LIFTING THE VEIL

*You are about to meet the most elegant, most lonely,
and most seductive Guardians of them all…*

Let me have the honour of introducing you to the denizens of a realm of mystery, legend and power. Within these pages you will be introduced to beings whose messages, expertise and commitment to guiding you is unsurpassed. For this world is now ready to be opened to us all, and these beings are ready to help – and be helped – by you.

The Vampires come to those who are undergoing a test. If a shadow has fallen over your life, if you are confronting the unknown, you may feel abandoned and lonely, as if there is no light, no guide, and no path to follow.

This is the time when we have need of those who walk the hidden paths of the Dark Forest, the ones who have made the Night their home, the guardians who can help you find your way back to the Dawn.

It is time for you to receive the support of the beautiful creatures called the Vampires.

**Who are the Vampires?**
Powerful, elegant and outcast, Vampires have been born, most often unwillingly, into a life which is dark and dangerous. To survive they have been urged again and again to give in to the most predatory aspects of Self. There have been many tales, many stories, and many half-told truths shared about them. Therefore, it is

natural to feel wary. But like many other otherworldly creatures, somehow human, yet completely "other", these beings are often misunderstood.

For they are creatures like us – they were once human, and walked in the Light. Unlike us they will not die: they are confined to evolving within one unchanging form. They also face, with unflinching awareness, a great test – to overcome their own hunger. The beings you will meet within these pages and depicted so richly in the paintings by Jasmine Becket-Griffith come from different places, times and cultures – but as Vampires, they are all complex and alluring, thrilling and powerful. They are often feared, and sometimes their isolation has led to great suffering and utter loneliness. They cannot see the light of the Sun, and must live on moonlight alone. But now, at this time, and through this book, they can be by your side, day or night, with their wisdom, their guidance, their teachings – born of experience. For you too are on the verge of life-changing lessons.

**Why would the Vampires help me?**
Vampires have had a noble quest assigned to them – and that is to serve Innocents. Innocents are human beings who are struggling with their own vulnerabilities, people who have been drained, in many ways, of their life force. To amend for some of their own former transgressions, The Children of the Night have received an assignment to help you – because in doing so, they will help themselves. They are abundant in all that you need at this time – rich in messages to offer, lessons to teach, and wisdoms to share with you. Be aware – Vampires are patient. They have all the time in the world. If they have been given a mission to care for you, and protect you, and assist you in a time of darkness, the Vampires won't give up. They will come to you, again and again with the express and only desire to be of assistance to you in Dark times now, and in Dark times ahead.

## Why work with the Vampires?

We learn languages best from a person who speaks the language and knows how to pronounce and shape the words. We learn a new sport best from someone who has practiced the same sport, who is familiar with all its nuances. We learn music best from those who play, and dancing from those who know the steps we wish to follow. The very best counsellors, mentors and guides in the human planes are those who have suffered the very same curses their clients bring to them to ease, heal and learn from. The school of experience is the very best there is. These Children of the Night have walked the same path you do now. They know this place, better than anyone. When it comes time to descend into the darkness it is far better to have by your side a guide who knows and understands the unfamiliar territory you have found yourself in – and one who has a clear mission, and a profound reason to help you.

## How will you know they are with you?

You will soon begin to receive messages, in very safe, secure ways from the Vampires within this book. They will literally light your way, helping you see what you could not see before. Masks will drop away from people and situations. You will be able to see the path that lies ahead, and you will have clear ideas, know the best action to take, and how to proceed. You will have an increased perception, be more aware of danger, or harmful influences, and know automatically who and what is worthy of your trust. Your timing and speed of reaction will greatly improve. You can begin to discern between healthy and unhealthy situations, places, people and choices – and if you have any doubt over the best course of action, the Vampires will step in and help you see even more clearly the potential future unwinding ahead of you.

As they are so powerfully gifted, your own clairvoyance, clairsentience, clairaudience and other intuitive abilities, including telepathy, will grow stronger, and become more accurate.

Because of their love of knowledge, the perfect books, teachers, courses and information will find you, effortlessly. Because they know what it is to be so very abandoned, they will help you see that no matter how insignificant you once may have felt, or how lost you now find yourself; you will find a home, and you will know you are worthwhile and that you matter. Above all, you will see that you are never alone.

**What the Vampires will help you with**
One of their wonderful attributes, because of their own struggle in overcoming their hunger, is that they can help you to overcome habits and traits that have held you back, or created illness, division and discord in your life. They also allow you to honestly undertake a kind of self-inventory, where you will forgive yourself for the seemingly harmful or selfish actions you may have taken throughout this lifetime. They will lift from you the self-hatred and the shame you have been so burdened with, and need live with no longer. They can help you release resentment and bitterness that is perpetuating harmful relationships, memories and patterns in your life. They will help you tap into your own vitality, and appreciate your simple, beautiful humanity.

They are Guardians – and one of their great talents is their ability to help you clear and free yourself from everyday sociopaths, bullies, victims, gossips and narcissists. You will begin to recognise toxic people and toxic traits, which drink and drain your life force. There are those who have not learned, and will perhaps never learn, how to generate their own energy – you will no longer allow them into your orbit. The Vampires will help you grow strong, and avoid these very people, and their efforts to take your energy away. The less contact you have with such people and situations, the more real and honest you become about your own vulnerabilities, and the stronger and brighter your own energy will shine. This will mean you have plentiful time, renewed energy and you will be full of inspiration to devote to people and projects you really care about – including yourself. Your priorities will shift, and life will feel more balanced, secure, joyful and fulfilling.

**How to use this book**
Think of this book as an oracle that you can turn to for messages of wisdom and guidance from the magickal creatures that grace its pages. Before consulting them, set aside some sacred space. This process can be as simple as lighting a white candle, and placing a circle of salt around it. As the candle burns down, the energy in your space will be cleared. You will feel a shift in the energy of the space almost immediately. You may even like to conduct a ceremonial blessing of your book, before you use it. I recommend lighting a little incense – Vampires adore frankincense which also has protective qualities, and will banish any negative energies or entities. When the smoke is billowing nicely, pass your book through once, twice, three times.

*"Vampires, of thee I ask*
*To help me now with this my task."*

Say thankyou to Great Spirit, The Universe, the God and the Goddess, and then let the incense stick or resin burn down.

You are now ready to consult the Vampires. Hold the book between your hands, close your eyes and think of a question for the oracle or a situation that you'd like to have some insight into. Then open the book randomly at any page, or flick through the pages until it feels right to stop. The vampires on the page you open to will have a powerful message for you to receive in that moment. Take time to connect with the beings in the images themselves as well as reading and reflecting on their message to you. It is time now for you to turn the page. To go forth and be met by your Dark Guardian, your protector. For you are now ready to receive the wisdom of the Vampires: The Children of the Night.

# ETERNAL YOUTH

The quest to remain young has never been more fervent than in your time. Everywhere we – and you – look, you will observe the obsession with being, and remaining line-less. Yet there are those who are young in their face and body, who are withered with age within their souls. Youthfulness cannot be found so much in the unwrinkled face, and the muscle without atrophy. The true youth is the one who never ceases to look at the world with wonder. The truly youthful human is the one who moves, breathes and lives with delight and fervour – with a sense of discovery. Those who have accepted imprisonment, order, stasis and the inevitability of slow corruption, who no longer engage the gifts of the mind and the body, as well as those whose spirits feel tired and jaded, who endlessly complain about ageing, and who compare themselves to images created by technology, are old before they need be. You can be eternally youthful by caring for yourself – this does not mean attempting to reverse ageing. It means embracing life. It means exploring the potential of your body and what it can do. It means doing what you love, not necessarily what is age-appropriate. It means having an attitude of joyful investigation into life. It means, we see, again and again, that those with curiosity for adventure, and renewal, are those who are youthful, even into their most vintage of years. Do not waste your human youth. Do not waste any of this blessed life you have been given.

# ENLIGHTENMENT

While a Vampire cannot walk in the sunlight, they are no strangers to various sources of light, and in fact adore candlelight, and the gentle glow of beeswax… they find that working and reading and contemplating by this light is soothing, reflective and comforting – especially when one is struggling to find answers to difficult dilemmas, as you are now. And so the answer will not come to you by daylight. It will come to you at night, and it will come to you by changing the source through which you expect enlightenment to arrive. In order to find an answer to the troubling issue at hand, you must first change the habits that have brought you this dilemma. You must switch the sources you go to for information. You must consider looking at the dilemma in a new and fresh way. And you ought best consider asking for assistance from one who has great experience with this kind of dilemma. You have until now, only sought justification as to why you should not have to endure this trouble – but there is an answer, and it is not in outrage, or denial, or avoidance. It is in seeking a fresh path through the forest, a light source unlike that of the sun, and advice from one who previously you were too proud to seek help from. The night has answers for you. Your shadows have the strengths you will need. Turn on a different source of light.

# KNOWLEDGE

Can you imagine what it would be like, to have a lifetime likely to stretch for one thousand years or more, to learn, to study and discover? For this is what we Vampires have – an eternity to study knowledge. The best of our kind take this miraculous opportunity to study, learn, and develop wisdom. And we can see that knowledge now seeks you. It is time to consider the great treasure houses of wisdom that exist in your world. It is time to step beyond being "entertained" by the trivial sideshow of mainstream television and entertainment – to cease sleepwalking through your life, and become aware of the decreasing span of your precious mortal days. Ask yourself, what is it you wish to learn? A language? To paint? To think, and to think well? To use your gift of the human mind? Perhaps medicine, herbalism, and other helpful sciences attract you. It is time, we say then, to know you have greater capacity to study and learn. It is time, to read, explore and learn more. Live, and die, and experience all you wish to – through the treasure of story and the treasury of knowledge that is books. This message can also indicate a need to ground your work, beliefs or knowledge with research. It is not always enough to simply "go within." Go within the souls of others too, and discover the incredible richness and potential of the human mind and expand yours too.

# ANCIENT

This ancient priestess sits amidst the bones of the past – she is the keeper of the secrets of the ancestors – and she raises the vessel from which she will drink the blood, and consume again the knowledge of the past. For this you do too – you turn to the blood knowledge you have within you, over and over, to guide you, heal you, give you strength in times of sorrow. How did I begin, you wonder, where are my forbears from? What part does my history play in my present? What part does the history of the ancestors play in my present? And how will my past shape the future? This message will often come up for humans who are adjusting to new information about members of their family – their heritage…the knowledge of what others have done, said, thought, felt, died of, been born into, is informing the present. You may be learning secrets about your family that have been kept for many years. And you will have with you a sense of the immortality of family lineage – that you are a part of the history of the planet, just as the plants and the trees are. Your family is the history of the planet – and it is time to acknowledge this and understand who you are, deep down, in the blood. And to find out which of this blood is wise, and which of this blood's influence can be overcome.

# NIGHTMARE

This Vampire speaks of the night which is restless, of the soul that cannot find the space in which to close their eyes and fully relax, whose dreams are creating agitation and distress, and who feels terror when knowing the darkness is falling, rather than the joy of the dark mother called night. For the night can be a place of terror for many – where the past repeats, old wars are fought, deep wounds reopen, and betrayal of yesteryear is as fresh a cut as if it took place that day. For in the dreamscape there is no time as we know it when we are awake – we are at the mercy of the consciousness and that energy we have with us, and all the hauntings of the world are nothing to the damnation of the twilight hours. If this is taking place for you or for another you care for, there is now a way for us to help you. This night-mare rider can enter your dreams. So fearless she is, and so fearsome her steed, that they will patrol the boundaries of your sleep, of your very dreams themselves. They will allow the gentler truths of your life to be recalled as you dream, and slowly, over time, the night will not hold such terror for you. Your dreams will become a safer place into which you can swoon each night, take your rest, and arise refreshed. This Night Mare and her Dark Rider will protect you. Dreams become beauty. Sleep becomes peace. Night is welcome, and the terrors of the past will change, when she rides forward, to guard your sleep.

# IMMORTAL

For many humans, we have noticed that their blood – and adopted friendship families can exert a draining and consuming influence upon them. We know this thing we once had, and which many of you have – Family – can from time to time strangle the development of the soul and the being. They can demand such great loyalty that you become entrenched in the family network, never moving beyond the ties of blood. This can be a diminishment of your potential, and we wish for you to consider that some of your beliefs have not been formed through your own independent experience, but have been fed to you, almost as mother's milk, or the blood we Vampires draw in from our prey. It is time for you to find aspects of who you could be, if dreams were given space to grow within. It is time to move beyond the demands and needs of family, even if it is for a short time, and refresh the freedom you have as one human, rather than as a cluster of close-knit and similarly woven humans who share a surname, or an interest. You must reassert your own individuality in healthy ways. For now, you must seek a form of freedom that comes from a separation, physical, emotional, mental, spiritual, from your family, their needs, their demands, the ties you have created yourself for a time.

# TRANSMISSION

There are those who cannot bear to be parted – and so, even if one has been infected with what you would call a negative – something that is likely to create difficulties and challenges in life – or even compromise life – some would rather share the negative experience than be parted by the possibility of two separate experiences. Thus we have a strange phenomenon. Who we spend our time with, who we share our lives with, is who we are very likely to become… we are special beings, even us, and we adapt and adopt – and become alike over time. It is as simple as observing that who you are with, who you spend your time with, who you choose to surround you, will have an influence on you. As your poet, John Donne said, "No man is an island." And so we sisters are here to tell you of the danger you are courting and the decision you must make. For you are either influencing another very strongly, or, another is influencing you and you would rather endure what some call hell than be separated by diverging experiences.

# SEDUCTION

This beautiful bed is the place where someone greeted their unspoken desire, and where they met their end. It is the place to which so many of you are drawn, even when you know the outcome may be dangerous. This Vampire comes to you now to warn you, empower you, and ask you to heed. The one who knows what it is you want, has a plan for you…and that plan involves their own satisfaction. It is not so simple and crass as sexual satisfaction, or a kind of food, or even a job or status in life you are being offered; it is the deep feeling that you are understood, accepted and desired for who you are. But it is a truth that this person who is now seducing you, is doing so with every kind of ability to stifle and inhibit your life force. This is not to say that you must look about you now with suspicion of all people – you must simply become aware of your desires, and your vulnerabilities. This message is a call to self-knowledge. To understand that when you are called to the beautiful bed, you may be drained, and you may even die to a part of yourself. For you will come to know that the love that has been offered to you, has been for the satisfaction of another. If you do go to the bed of the Vampire, you will leave a part of yourself there. Someone about you is ready to seduce you. If you choose to be seduced, they will have what they want, and you will lose more than you know. Be careful.

# CREATOR

You are the Creator of yourself. Each day with your thoughts, actions and decisions you create anew the form your natural energies and soul will take. This is what we wish to say to you now. You can recreate yourself. You may choose to live in the light, or in the dark. You are being reminded of your responsibility as a creator – you have created an idea, perhaps even given birth to a new one of your kind, just as this Vampire alchemist has created the tiny deer she will feed with a vial of transforming blood. You are the vessel through which new life and ideas are born. As a creator, you are responsible for those you make. You must see through the time after they are born. You must nurture the young ones, be they ideas or projects or real, living beings. You must also teach them, and train them, and let them know how to survive. You must be sure they have those essential skills only you can teach them – and teach them well. You must also love them, despite their imperfections. You must find within you that great reservoir of love that even we Vampires never lose, that human part of us that never leaves us, and keeps us ensoulled.

# HER LAST DAY IN THE LIGHT

There are many times in your human life when you walk for the last time in a circumstance or situation, which you take very much for granted. But we are here to share with you news both good and bad – the news that a time is coming to an end, and a great source of security may be about to finish for you – and it will soon be your turn to have a hardship that only you can bear, and become heroic in the undertaking. There is no cause for you to fear, though being human, you will fear. It is time to understand more of what you have avoided and what circumstance soon to come to you will teach you. You will not lose anything that you cannot bear – although it is a sacrifice and it shall be difficult, and at times, you will struggle. But this ending must take place for you to come to even greater illumination at a later time, and for the angelic nature within you to grow, you must endure something that will temper you, as the finest sword of the Archangel Michael. You will become again one who walks in the miracle of the light, of colour, of the creatures who live amongst the rays of light that stream from the noble sun. You will emerge. And all about you will be the Miracle of Day, of Light, after the great darkness.

# DEATH RITES

For many beings, the reality of death seems to be the ultimate cruelty – the Vampire that steals the life from so many – and without, it seems, any order or reality. For death it is true visits us all, whether we are young, or old, or healthy, or suffering …for all of us, beast and beauty, there is a time for the end to come. But there are angels of death, appointed by the universe to help us move from one side, to the next…and to avoid staying in between, without moving on, transforming. For the soul who dies well, who has a good death, there is a transformation through the realms that divide the living from the dead. For this to take place, the angels of death do not only come to assist the soul, but they assist with the ones left behind. And what comforts those who remain on the earth are rites, ways to say goodbye, honourings and reverence, and memories and mirth. It may be time for you to consider those who have gone from you, or who may go – and know how you would honour them, and remember them, and send them on their way. Consider what will comfort you when you are on your way too – know that it is not morbid to contemplate the ending of this mortal time for you. There is so much beyond that last breath, that last glimpse of light of the sun – so the angel of death assures us.

# CALL FOR HELP

Often, you humans have an unerring ability to sense when we are around. When there is danger. When there is something not quite right. Something amiss. And yet over and over you smother this feeling, this intuitive gift you all have. But at this time, you are able to discern when there is a shift in the atmosphere. When something is about or around you. It is pre-sentience, and it is clear. And when this Vampire comes to you, we say, your senses are correct, they are natural, and they are good, and it is time to share this feeling with a trusted friend or person in authority who can help. It is time to remove yourself from an atmosphere of danger, to understand that you are not weak for seeking help, and that further confirmation is not required. All you need to do is ask for assistance, and it will come. No more looking over your shoulder. No more doubting your very real, very worthwhile sixth sense. Trust it. And take steps to make yourself safe and comfortable. Remove untrustworthy people. Be cautious in your dealings. Lift your shields, and stand with an ally and friend. Dare to take your own premonition seriously.

# PRIMAL

When you move, you say so many things about yourself. The way you hold your body, the way you inhabit your form, and the way you speak with your physical self is pure communication. Your energy is within your physicality, and it reaches out through you, and you have a conversation with the whole world through this language of the body. As modern people, you forget this – and you tend to move as though your minds are living a separate life to your bodies. When you dance, you are asked to become your deeper, older, more animistic self. Dance is an expression of health, personality, emotions and of your nature – your natural self. There is a difference between when humans dance and when the Vampires do... when humans dance, and when they dance deeply, from a place where they are unselfconscious and as if they are unwatched, or care not if they are watched – they are deeply, incomparably beautiful. When they dance with their whole souls, they are primal. This is what you must do now. Reconnect with that most instinctual of places. Go deep into your flesh, and dance the story of your life. Forget all, except for the movement, and the bliss, and the healing it will give you. This primal movement will be the greatest blessing for you, at this time. A way to at once forget your troubles, and remember who you truly are.

# COMPASSION

There are times in our life when circumstances, and people, and what we see have a certain horror to them. It is the horror of being unable to believe that there is such cruelty, and malice, and injustice in the world. Each day, if we allow ourselves, we expose our minds, and our hearts and energies, to events that hold enough tragedy within them for us to suffer pain on behalf of other humans, animals, and all the fellow creatures we share this planet with. We children of the night know this suffering too, and sometimes cannot bear to stand it a moment longer. We have no more forbearance at times, and that is when we step forward, and carry those who are suffering so very deeply. When this Vampire appears to you, know that even the unlikeliest hearts hold compassion, and sometimes, they cannot bear the suffering about them, any more than you can. And they become an ally, comforting those who have fallen, who are unable to rise and take steps towards the rebirth of their own life. Rest now, and allow them to carry you for a time.

# REASON

I am the one who comes to you now so you can see clearly! You feel others have had problems in this area, but if you simply think positively and send out waves of love the way will be cleared. But no, this is not how this particular power works, my friend. There is an obstructive force around you at present, one that will not allow you to pass, unless you strictly meet all criteria. This force, in the form of a person, or institution, or corporation requires you to do everything that is required to pass through the gates. How do I know this? I am one of them, and have been one of them, and will continue to be the gatekeeper for many activities. I am a Queen, and I choose who enters the gateways of immortality in my realm, and for all those who dare climb the path to my lair, there are many who are turned away... and they are the fortunate ones. Take care. Be aware. And do everything, as if you were writing with your very blood, and it was your soul you were selling.

# THE CALL OF THE NIGHT

You have of late fallen into patterns that are soothing in their regularity. You know what to expect, and when to expect it. You are surrounded by respect and acceptance, and you are widely loved and applauded. You are content. You are comfortable, and have no real reason to become otherwise. I say to you now, I was once like you. And then, the night and her darkness called me. I changed, and I left behind the world of daylight, and for a time I travelled from my loved ones, although some chose to travel with me. I departed from all that I knew in so many ways, and in doing so, I became more perfectly myself than if I had stayed in that perfectly still, comfortable place. For in the testing, I was reborn. For in the challenge, I was forged. And in the loneliness, I came to know myself. This time is one which I can only partake of, truly, alone. And for you, you fear leaving the comfort zone. You prefer all that is known. But I tell you, that with this message comes the Call of the Night, and of her wild creatures. What it will teach you, and offer you, is more valuable and strange than you can imagine. And the adventure will leave you feeling more alive, your every sense tingling, more than ever before.

# THE PAST A PRISON

We warn you now, of the motives of another who insists on telling their tragic story to you, over and over, until you have lost part of your soul to them, and wish to defend them. Heed our message: this is not your battle to fight, nor your story to live. You have your own path, and you will have your own tragedies. Yes, you can support another, with time, your care, and lend a hand. But they wish none of these things – they wish your full consumption by their story – and they will condemn you if you do not immerse yourself in their long past issue. Watch – and see if they wish you to re-enact their issues. And if so – then beware, and do your best to live your story, and to distance yourself from this one, who will ask you to deny your own story, and live out their own, again and again, until you forget your self, and become a shadow of who you were always intended to be. Do not make someone else's past your prison.

# ANTI-HERO

Most people are trained to recognise what looks good – from appearances, the kind of jobs people have, and the way you humans even walk and talk. And the person, the human being you are, is something that cannot be identified and classified simply, but the truth is that you have done a very good thing. You are a safe person, a good one, we can sense this from you, and we wish to acknowledge the valour and the brightness that surrounds you. The deed that you have done will not be recognised as soon as you would wish, but the impact it has will ripple out through the energy of the world, and in return, you will be noticed by many, many who also will never quite fit in, or be recognised despite the good they do. All are the sum of their actions, and their choices within their circumstances. Even the roughest and most humble among us can become the hero, and those who are greatest and most seen to do good, often are glorying in their own virtues. Do not fear. You are a walker of the night, and yet, your time will come. You will inspire love. You are more than those who cannot see you, say you are. Their voices are empty. Your life, although strange, is full.

# MAENAD

Maeneds are the female priestesses of the God Dionysus, maddened by the fruits of the vine, and given the space of ritual, they descend into an ecstasy, where an orgy of carnal delights, instability, frenzied dance, and gluttony are all allowed and celebrated. Within that space, the divine madness we all have – including you – is given expression, and exhausts itself, relatively safely. When she comes to you, it is for you to now find a safe space to do what you have considered to be unsafe, in a safe and protected way. You may be longing to be free, wild and to let loose…to cast off the chains and find expression in dancing, sex, parties, and intoxication… and she comes to you now, this creature who will devour you if you do not find a way to safely express these urges. For that is vampiric – the urge to express the divine madness that will erode your soul if you repress it any longer – and that is when the vampiric maenad can tear you to pieces. That is when addiction can find you. This is when over-indulgence can stake its claim on your soul through your physical form. It is time for joy to be lived through you. It is time for madness. It is time to drink the nectar of love making, wine, laughter to the point where your belly hurts… it is time.

# REDEMPTION

Penitence is a kind of healing, so you are being shown clearly that you need to feel the relief of saying sorry. This penitence is not made to burden or punish the self, but to relieve the self from the negative impact of imbalanced action, thoughts and words. It hurts us when we hurt another. It is a form of self-abuse to indulge a momentary urge for spite, or selfishness, or greed, because you will pay for that, over and over. And you resist the apology, you do, for we have seen it. You fight the need to say, "I can do better." For you can. You truly can. And to admit to such is not to take blame or be made wrong, for anyone wishing to do this to you is not a pure soul. But for you to recognise a misdeed, and to affirm you are better than that, by saying "I am sorry," this is a humble, beautiful, strengthening thing. To say sorry, is to be redeemed from the self-hatred, the judgment, and the silent criticism that otherwise repeats throughout your mind. Be what you are: sorry. Repent, but do not punish yourself. Be sorry for the right reasons – this is not 'sorry' for being human, for loving, for making a mistake. It is sorry for hurting another who expected that you be your best self. And what that best self is, is what you must decide, and aim to become.

# THIRST

You are currently craving something with such a great thirst that it is dominating your thoughts and feelings and you can think of hardly anything else. Thirst can be wonderful when that which you long for, yearn for, is healthy and wise – but in this case, the thirst is for the kind of experience you know will have life-changing consequences. For with us, the thirst we experience is not just for the blood, the drink that sustains us, it is for the stream of humanity and the song of life and beautiful warmth that runs through the blood. So too for you: what you thirst for is very close to becoming an addiction, or an obsession which draws you away from what makes you, you. If it is a person you thirst for, their touch, their love, or if it is a substance, know that this thirst is exerting a powerful force, even close to a control. There may be an addiction, or an addictive way of thinking and feeling working its way into your life. We wish to direct your consciousness to this thirst, and ask you to question its source – what is it the thirst craves? Can it be satisfied? Or are you simply compelled to search and drink again and again. Know that some thirsts can be satisfied in ways that are in tune with your personality, your 'self' this time, all manifestations of your essence and soul. And others will steal you further and further away from your true self.

# OUTSIDER

You, like us, feel estranged from the human world at the moment. It is as if a glass separates you from others, and their world. You look at the lives of others, and there is a sense of mild regret at how distant it all seems. You feel unable to find the true meaning in anyone else's experience, and you cannot relate to what so many people care about. You do not know what it is you will do for the rest of your human days. You feel an outsider, looking ever inwards, but not feeling a part of any community, or group, or even any family. At this time, strange as it can be, disorienting as it can be, you are wondering about your human-ness, if indeed you really belong to this great, thriving, greedy, enormous, wise and childish family called the human race. This estrangement is current, but it is not eternal. Still, there will always be something of the orphan child about you, even if you have never suffered the abandonment so many have. You simply are different, and you have yet to find your own kind. And the truth is that when you do find your own kind, you and they may only be able to be with each other in unusual, unconventional ways, or for shorter lengths of time.

# FREE WILL

One of the ironies of the vampiric life is that many of us who have become this unnatural, yet very much alive creature did not choose to become this way. We were turned, created, transformed, and often against our will. And so we wish to speak to you of the sacred nature of free will, of consent. Your free will, and the free will of others is sacred. If one is taken and transformed, a dreadful bond is created, and one which must be paid for, most often with pain. For to transgress the wishes of another is against the laws we have developed to keep us from falling too deeply into an abyss of depravity and cruelty. If you have had something occur against your will, you will feel something of your soul's vitality draining from you, for the soul needs its blood, its chi, nwyfre, prana, too. It may be unseen, but the angels can glimpse it, as can those of you with the preternatural sight. Free will is as sacred as a sacrament in the Church, and to you, this is very important at present. If one has stolen fragments of your soul through the imposition of their will upon your own, strengthen your will at this time. Do not go with the flow, as they say – for this is an energy imposed by culture, or by another soul, who loves to have the energy of those who follow them at their disposal.

# LOVE CONQUERS ALL

Some love endures only until a change comes to visit. And then that love, that connection, the friendship can dissolve. Some friendships and connections are strong and healthy, only to die due to neglect, or because one partner shifts an alliance to another. But in the heart of these creatures, these faithful ones, we can see a love and a commitment that truly is enduring. For we have experienced it, just as this new Vampire is experiencing it within this image. From one lifetime to the next, through transformation, they will come to greet her. They know she is changed. They can sense her difference. But they are hers, and she is theirs, and that bond is unbreakable, until true death takes them away from each other, and even then, the love endures through memory and the presence that lingers after death. For there is a love that endures beyond distance, change, and radical shifts in energy and circumstances. There are those who are faithful, and to whom you have given your bond. There is a love and faithfulness that endures, even beyond lifetimes. This is yours. Observe this miracle of everlasting trust and love. Be grateful. And give thanks.

# THE MONSTER WITHIN

There is something we know more about than anyone could ever imagine. We are afraid never of the world, but of our ability to destroy something tender and beautiful within an instant, because our very nature ensures we hunger for something that will kill those we love if we take it. This is a terrible dilemma, for we are loveable, and loving – we know how to draw close, and how to be well, and in control, for many years. But at some time, in a moment of weakness, when defences are down and we hunger and our humanity is far away, we may snap, and our hunger may overrun the incredible control and balance we've had. We would never hurt you. And yet, our urge to love you is tied up with our urge to have you. We must learn vast powers of discipline. And this is what can lead us to vanish from the lives of those we care most for. If you have opened the book to this page, it would seem you too are struggling with an aspect of yourself that you know can bring harm to another, but which is a natural part of you – you are wrestling the demons that lie within.

# JEALOUSY

Your desire to care for your own, your blessings and what you love has attracted envy from others. This has sparked guilt and fear within you. And now you are in danger of punishing yourself simply because another wishes you to be hurt. Instead of suffering, you can change. And you can become strong, even when there are those who wish to harm you, and who are powerful. Learn from Lamia's serpent self – the serpent is the Divine Feminine, and a being who sheds skin, mothers fiercely and who can feel the faintest of changes in energy and vibration. You too can sense the slightest change at the moment. You are able to anticipate any threats and any danger. She is unable to close her eyes – so her gift to you is to have your eyes wide open, to observe all the changes and to be honest about what you are undergoing. She is a strong creature for you to have chosen – and if she has come to you, you have the ability to stay fierce, protect what you love, and connect with the Divine Feminine. It may also be that there is gossip about your appearance, and your sexual behaviour. Call those who speak against you out, name them, and declare yourself free. Do not allow anyone to question your behaviour when it is their own actions they are choosing to overlook.

# ECSTASY

The connection so many have with others who are vampiric in nature is that the giving up of will, and of force, and of being submissive towards another is a way of experiencing a kind of ecstasy. It is not a lack of power that enables you to experience this – to become soft and yielding, and to allow the will of another who is worthy to dominate is an experience of surrender. It is not helpless, or about giving up – it is a choice, for a time, to allow your own will to be dominated by the will of another – and in this experience, ecstasy can be found. Now it is time for the deep relaxation and restoration…to allow one about you, who is worthy, to give to you in ways that create an ecstatic experience, and a deep bond of trust. When we take a lover, when we fall in love, so deeply and passionately as we do, the ecstatic response of our beloved to our kiss, touch, words, is our greatest gift and our greatest pleasure. This we wish you to experience. But only with one worthy of your beautiful surrender.

# BURNT BY THE SUN

There are times when you have set yourself a great task – when you have decided that you have within sights a glorious outcome. It could be an ambition, or a relationship, or a position, or an achievement. But there is a warning – a caution to you. There is much that can come to you simply and with ease – but there are things in this world, which we both share, that must be earned. You must earn this next step. And there is a path to walk, and a road to take before you can get there. You may of course decide that we do not know of what we speak, or of you, and your desire – and you may decide to reach as high as you can. And we say to you, when this sun you reach for burns you with its fire – for it is a star and made of fire – you will learn then what it is to be too eager, too soon. There is a time, and a place, and a way in which we earn what will be ours. The desire is worthy of you. You are worthy of reaching it. But for now, the dream, which you reach for, you are not yet ready for. There is more work for you to do first. Be wise.

# WITNESS

Vampires like us, we are said not to exist. But you know there is more here on this planet than anyone can even begin to dream of. You know we are true. And you have witnessed something of late that others still deny is "real." But you are now a witness and having seen, you cannot un-see. Knowing, you can no longer deny. It is not that we wish for you to tell all of your new knowledge. It is that we wish you to not lie to yourself, to no longer agonise over questions of whether what you saw and felt and understood is true or untrue. There is so much on this planet of ours. Think of it. And you and I, though so different, are between us only two types of the millions of variations on the extraordinary creatures there are. Who is either of us to deny the truth of the wonder that is this planet and all the manifestations of life upon it? You have seen what some say is untrue. Know that it is not a lie. It would be a lie and harmful to you to deny what you know after the gift of this knowledge.

# THAT DEATH WILL COME

One day, as all of us must, you will die. What do these words strike into you? Fear? Resolution to live? Acceptance? Or is there simply a sense of what is not known? We have lived longer than humans, yet we are not so old as the cycle of life. We too will come to our ending, and we, just as you, do not know for certain what will take place. Will there be a void, an emptiness? A nothingness? Will there be peace? Will there be punishment? But one thing we can be sure of. There will be an ending. Those who tell you they know for sure what lies on the other side, believe them not. Because when we live, that is what we know. Your mortality is beautiful. Of it is born compassion. The desire to live well and deeply. In the brevity of human spans is the impetus that drives you to explore, to go further, and to create rich experience. In the full understanding of your mortality and its beauty, you will begin to explore the potential of being alive, now. It matters not if you have many more lives to live, have lived before, or will live again. All that matters is now, and what you do with every moment you are blessed with.

# PREY

We have come to tell you that there is one who sees you as prey, and they see themselves as the hunter. And the more they can persuade you that you wish to play this role, and that it is your fault, the more powerful they will become. This Vampire comes forth when one has been groomed to be hurt. There are many examples of abuse and monstrosity in your world, amongst humans. And often it is the one who is most close to you, who will take what is most precious to you. Do not become prey. And do not agree to this hunter being invited by you. The victimisation they are visiting upon you has not been invited by you, except through circumstance. There is no contract that means this must play out. If you feel this is wrong, speak up, and speak out. Being hunted, being preyed upon, is not something you must take the responsibility for, nor must this play out. You can change the script in the hunter's head. You can change the outcome. You can refuse to become prey. You can play this game quite differently to the script they have handed you. In fact, you need not play the part at all.

# HUNTER

For you to live each day, something must die. Be it for the food on your table, or the produce that has become your walls and the home you live in, energy has given up one form and become another. Everything transforms. But for that which you seek now, the hunt needs to go within. The chase must be of that part of your character which, when hunted down and integrated, will give you what you lack in order to create what you need. You need to become the hunter of the hidden parts of your own self, of the courage you feel you lack, of the opportunity you believe you have not been given. For you breathe, do you not? And as you breathe, you, a part of you, is the hunter, and must take action to obtain what it is you long for. No one else will do this for you. This task is yours alone, human.

# REBELLION

There is about you an established order. There is about you a power that says things must be done in a particular way. That the order is rightful, and must be maintained. The freedom to question is being refused, and is considered to be offensive. The right to speak up, even respectfully, is being restrained. Those who find a new way to approach the old problems are considered dangerous. And for a time, now, you have kept silent. But there is a different way – many different ways – of approaching the same questions. Instead of each person having the right to approach the questions in a way that is true to them, you are being asked not to think, not to feel, but simply to follow. And you are tired of following when this following is taking you no closer to the adventures and solutions you wish to discover. But it is hard to be the one who speaks up. It is challenging to be the one to say there may be another way. For to do so in your place right now is to become a rebel. This sounds romantic, but it is not. It is a hard path to walk, yet it is the one you are being asked to set off on.

# DISCIPLINE

You want something to be easier than it must be in order for you to value it. You want something to happen faster than it can for your own growth and stability. You are, in short, much like most humans we see. You lack discipline. There are times when we feel that in order to achieve something, or to reach a goal, we need only meditate upon it, visualise it as being real, and it will therefore come to us through the process you have come to call The Law of Attraction. There is another law. The law of contribution and hard work and tenacity. It has no pretty name. It offers no quick fix. But it is real and its results are lasting and true. And this is the lesson with you at present. There is a desire within your culture to at all times experience happiness and comfort. It has created generations of people who are physically unwell, mentally lazy, and spiritually apathetic. The discipline that is being required of you will result in a great breakthrough. You know that a major part of your life requires a change, and the brutal truth, which we give you here, is that this will be hard. You must not wait for motivation and desire. You must commit, and build the discipline to carry through this plan that will see so many blessings able to enter your life. Carving out the doorway will take willpower, action, and showing up, again and again.

# SACRIFICE

It is time for you to examine what you value most, and what you would least wish to give up. The word 'sacrifice', and we know this as we have lived long, is a way of making the thing you give up sacred. It is a loss. It is painful. It matters. Therefore the void that is left means something, and must be filled with something that means more. For so many of you, you will not choose. You wish to be good to all. You wish to let down none. You do not think about what is best. For what is best is that which sets your blood alight, and makes the song of your soul soar. What is best is that you know your own heart, and know your own code, and adhere as closely as possible to what is noble about you. There will not be time for all, space for all, love for all. You may protest – you may wonder, what of loving everyone unconditionally? But that is an illusion. Even in love, you must choose. So, we say now, you must sacrifice something. You must give up something that is precious. By doing so, make it beautiful. Make it worth it. Make it count. And make this deliberate. Do not play victim. Make your choice, and be powerful and compassionate at once.

# FAITH

The belief that something will take place, or is right, or is a particular way, can be called faith. Faith is quiet and hopeful, offers contentment and calm, it has not bravado, and it need not insist on its rightness. Faith is something we have too, and we observe it in the best of those we call humans, the warm-blooded ones of whom you are one. It is a beautiful gift that you humans have to be believers in this quiet, gentle way. Faith is not always beautifully expressed. Faith is a loving, amazing quality, but it must be attached to something that is worthwhile. At this time, it is best to examine what it is you have faith in. What is faith to you? Were you taught faith as a child, and did you lose faith at one point? For you are often taught to believe in things that do not deserve your faith. It may now be time to relearn what it is you have enduring constant hope for – what you know will come to be, even if your eyes may never see it. And we know about Faith… the persistent notion that all will be well in time. For we live with this faith. Without it, we would be dead inside. The human spirit has faithfulness at its core, at its best. To have faith is to remain loyal, but in a truly heartfelt way. Tender, moving and full of grace, your faith may soon return to you. Choose wisely in what you place this gift of your faith.

# RELIGION

Religion has been through so much with you humans. We have watched it change, moment to moment it would seem. Every thousand years or so your Gods have changed, your faiths have changed, and people everywhere have died, again and again, for the rightness of all you say is right and true. Yet we wonder at this thing called religion. For you have made vows not only in this life. You can recall the lives of long ago, and at times, there are vows and structures you have carried with you from life to life, the tattered remnants of belief and the sharp knives of punishment follow you, lifetime after lifetime, and all the while you say, I am not religious. I am spiritual. But you are religious. You are and have been so much, so many things, and religion has been drunk in at your mother's breast and formed so much of who you are. Become aware, we say, of this. No longer deny this, we ask. For you, unlike us, will be born again and again, and when you understand what it is this framework of understanding the world has given to you – and what it has also stolen from you – you will come to a place where your own soul has room to breathe. For religion, and religious beliefs may have given humanity purpose and survival strategies – but they have simultaneously suffocated the true expressions of their souls. It is a vast form of black magick. And we have all dabbled in it. It is time to wash it clean – but first, we must know what it is we have, what no longer helps us, and what we choose to believe and become, from this day forth.

# COURTESY

Manners are not simply a façade to veil our cruelty, or the terrible hunger that creates that cruelty. Manners are a way of gracefully doing what must be done, to smooth the difficulties we all must face, and to create beauty amongst days that can be full of crude squalor. Having manners is to think of others' comfort, and what will please them. This message we bring to you this day speaks to you of the need under the current circumstances to speak the truth, but to do so with grace and diplomacy and the least offence possible. This means to work out what it is you wish to achieve in the forthcoming discussions, and how to best appease the offence, which has already flared. With manners, diplomacy and thoughtfulness, you may still navigate this treacherous stretch of your life. It is worth being kind, truthful, and yet graceful. The time has come to marry up grace, with truth, and consideration. Use the beautiful, magickal gift of your good sense, and your charm, and watch doors open, and problems dissolve with newfound understanding.

# SUPERNATURAL

There are many things in the world that most people cannot explain away conveniently. That includes Vampires. Like this beautiful silver haired creature surrounded by flying fish as the sun breathes its last behind her. Before her is a surreal vision. And yet, there it is. Real, yet unreal at the same time. And we are scientists and we are doctors and we teach and we walk amongst you. And we hear so many times of what is said to be impossible: the hearing of thoughts. The moving of objects through energy. The knowing of events before they occur. The receiving of messages from Spirit realms. The ability to see colours around bodies. The ability to heal through touch. And I tell you all that these are not 'supernatural'. They are natural. And when they are developed and worked upon, and exercised and practiced with, they are considered super. You have these qualities. You have them in abundance. And we can see them about you. It is your task now to develop them. Not to develop them without reason and intelligence – but to develop them and to celebrate your nature, your magnificent humanity which has such potential, and which is so vital to all of us. You are supernatural. You are as magnificent as those who are in spirit. You are a divine creation. And it is now time for you to celebrate this, to embrace this, and to become as strong in your extra senses as you are in others. Embrace yourself, human child. All of your magickal, wondrous self.

# NATURAL

To be your own true self is a lifelong – lifetimes long – purpose. It is the purpose of this existence, and for each of us, despite the labels we all have – human, vampire, woman, man. We have something greater at play – how the essence, that very drop of pure self makes itself known through us. And for this great miracle to take place, there are habits to be shed, reactions to be questioned, challenges to be met, and experiments to be made. For you are not who you have been told you are. And so we ask for you to clearly and finally, perhaps understand and acknowledge that all that you are can be discovered when you take yourself within, and quietly feel, look and listen to your own self. Not the self of the label, the job. Not the defences you have developed for protection. Not the protests of ego, or the demands of family voices within. It is who you truly are. And then, once having found a sense of that, to live from that place in small, consistent ways each day. How that manifests will be unique for each of you. But we ask for you now to go beyond the labels of time, and place, and family, and education, and status – and go deep, deep within. There is something within you that is more than the history of others. That is yours alone. And the world needs it to be expressed – otherwise, why would you have been created?

# TRANSGRESSION

The most perfected souls upon this planet have all created moments in their lives where they have gone against their own values, and their own hearts, their own souls…and transgressed. They have hurt themselves, as they have hurt others. It is incorrect of you to assume that your faults and flaws, your poor decisions, and yes, the mistakes you have made are more ghastly than any other. There is not one amongst any of us who has not done wrong. And it is good that we Vampires and you humans can feel remorse, and take steps to correct ourselves, and do better. But to continually internally erode your own value due to another's encouragement is a false kind of virtue. There is no good in hurting yourself, over and over, to prove how sorry you are. Live better, do better, but let the self-punishment go, and do not allow another to utilise your compassionate remorse for their own ends. Yes, they are. We are all – human, and otherworld creature – going to transgress against the natural laws and the laws of our own souls. What we do about it is what matters. Go on now and make amends, then give thanks for the gift of self-forgiveness.

# NOBILITY

You have shown nobility of spirit, and action, and you have behaved in a manner which has drawn our attention. We wish to encourage you to behave in these noble ways more often. Nobility is a sense of innate virtue, or being able to do what is best and right within circumstances that would have been easier had we simply fallen into step with the prevailing thinking. You have helped the helpless. You have protected one who was weaker. You have spoken for the voiceless. You have been virtuous with no thought of reward. But this is the reward you did not ask for, but deserve. For you are as a Knight, or Lady, in the most chivalrous of tales, and you have lived with grace, and are becoming a more refined being with every day. We wish to honour you now, and say, you have done well. Accept the acknowledgement. And know that the good deeds you have done so selflessly will ripple out into the world, and make changes you may never see, but your soul will know you made all the difference to one who was helpless, and to whom you gave your aid. We honour you, noble Sir, noble Lady.

# HOPE

This little creature, this small one, a Vampire with a heart and soul, is surrounded by death. By endings. By sadness. By the void. And by those who have left her. Like you, she is facing the darkness within others and within life, and she feels utterly alone. But what she has with her is the ability to hope. And she chooses this. It is not something that is always easy, but she has lit a candle in the deep darkness, upon a heap of skulls and nothing else, and she has struck a light, and held up the light. She is quietly defiant in the face of death, of change, of silence, of loneliness, of criticism, and of a great dilemma. At this time, you are being asked to rise above those who are giving in to hopelessness and negativity. We do not ask you to be falsely hopeful, or to put on a happy face and refuse to face what must be faced. We ask you to be hopeful. You do not yet know the outcome. You do not yet know what will next happen. But what you can be assured of is that this hope that you have the capacity to create will sustain you in a time of great difficulty. Keep it strong, quiet, small even. Face what you must face. Do what must be done. And know that yes, this situation is very difficult. No doubt about it at all. But we Vampires ask you to know that one of the most beautiful and life-affirming things any of us can do is refuse to give in, and not only that, to do what must be done with hope. That light will attract help, intervention, assistance, and our admiration and respect, which in turn will deliver more assistance.

# RESURRECTION

You have almost given up on yourself. Almost lost touch with your enthusiasm for life. You have thought sometimes, maybe this is it, and found some kind of comfort in what you call acceptance. But we are here to show to you that in front of you, right at your feet, right in this moment, is the chance you have secretly dreamed of for so long. You have the chance to completely change your life. And if you choose to take up the offer, of your life being remade and renewed, be assured that the very best of yourself, that never had the chance for expression before, will now have its moment. But it requires that you arise, shake off the past, and start again. You have so much more to do, to give, to become – put away all thoughts that your life was static and decided upon. You have forgiven yourself. Now you must remake your own life. This is a wonderful time to look for a new job, make important changes in your home with renovations, or move countries, change career, and even change your appearance – naturally, of course. Everything you need to revive and continue with renewed optimism and energy is with you at this time. The Vampires, the experts on new life, confirm that it is so. You are about to rise again. And those who will be surprised, will be inspired to change their own lives in the places that need it most.

# ABOUT THE AUTHOR

**Lucy Cavendish** works magick every single day of her life, embracing it as a creed for personal fulfillment and happiness, and as a belief system that sees us as part of nature, and thus gives us all the motivation to respect and revere and delight in our unique experience here on Planet Earth.

Some of Lucy's other bestselling publications include *Oracle of the Dragonfae*, *Les Vampires Oracle*, *Oracle of Shadows & Light*, *Oracle of the Mermaids*, *Oracle of the Shapeshifters*, *Wild Wisdom of the Faery Oracle* and *The Lost Lands*.

Apart from regular television and radio appearances, she is a feature writer for 'Spellcraft Magazine', 'Spheres', and has appeared in anthologies like 'Disinformation's Pop Goes The Witch!' In 1992, Lucy created Witchcraft magazine, which she edited for five years.

She is a classic book witch and adores writing, reading and creating enchanted workshop experiences. Lucy Cavendish currently lives in Sydney with her pixie-like daughter and the spirit of her beautiful labradoodle dog.

Visit Lucy's website at: **www.lucycavendish.com**

# ABOUT THE ARTIST

**Jasmine Becket-Griffith** is a world-renowned fantasy artist. Born in 1979, she has spent all of her adult life working as a fine artist, painting traditionally by hand with acrylic paints. Her artwork can be found in private collections and public displays throughout the world. Jasmine's paintings blend realism with wide-eyed wonder – exploring gothic themes, with elements of classical literature, the occult, nature and fantasy – and of course, faeries!

Jasmine's paintings appear in countless books (notably *The World of Faery* with Alan Lee, *The Art of Faery* with Brian Froud, *Spectrum 11*, *Spectrum 13*, *Gothic Art Now*, *Big Eye Art: Resurrected and Transformed* and her four solo art books *Strangeling: The Art of Jasmine Becket-Griffith*, *Fairy*, *Jasmine Becket-Griffith: Porfolio Volume I* and *Portfolio Volume II*). Her work also graces many television shows and movies, magazines and advertisements, tattoo parlours, themeparks, and of course her range of hundreds of different licensed merchandise products (distributed chain stores such as Hot Topic, Torrid, and Target/Super Target) as well as lines of collectibles through the Bradford Exchange and Hamilton Collection. Jasmine's official website and online gallery can be seen at www.strangeling.com and she also has an eBay store under the seller ID 'strangeling'.

Jasmine lives in beautiful Celebration, Florida with her husband/assistant Matt and their cats.

For more information on this
or any Blue Angel Publishing release,
please visit our website at:

**www.blueangelonline.com**